WITHDRAWN

A GUIDE TO
CHURCH PLANTING

A GUIDE TO
CHURCH PLANTING

By

MELVIN L. HODGES

MOODY PRESS
CHICAGO

© 1973 by
THE MOODY BIBLE INSTITUTE
OF CHICAGO

ISBN: 0-8024-3380-4

Second Printing, 1974

Library of Congress Catalog Number:
73-7334

Printed in the United States of America

DEDICATION

*To my wife, who has been a constant source
of encouragement and inspiration in the rewarding
task of establishing the church on foreign soil*

Contents

Preface

"PERHAPS the greatest problem of conservative evangelical mission strategy is not whether or not the planting of responsible churches is the central task, but rather *how these churches can be successfully planted*" (italics added). So stated Frank Severn in a paper on "How to Plant a Responsible Church" presented at a seminar on Church Planting and Development, held at Trinity Evangelical Divinity School in June 1970.

In this present effort, I am undertaking to continue a task begun in *The Indigenous Church*.[1] In that book, I attempted to show the biblical basis and the practical application of the three main thrusts of the indigenous church principles: self-government, self-propagation, and self-support. Here I am enlarging upon the practical steps in church planting. I am acutely aware that it is impossible to give a how-to-do-it guide to church planting as though the process could be mastered in six easy lessons! Awareness of the necessity of a fresh approach to each new circumstance and of the indispensability of the personal guidance of the Holy Spirit in carrying out *His* work would preclude any attempt to present church planting as a mechanical process. Yet there are practical lessons to be learned from both the Scriptures and experience which can be shared with others and result in increased success in the challenging task of church planting. My prayer is that this will be so.

1. Springfield, Mo.: Gospel Publishing, 1953.

9

Introduction

THE THEOLOGICAL FOUNDATION for continuing to plant churches has come under attack in the contemporary debate concerning the mission of the church to the modern world. A few extremists proclaim that God is dead. By this they mean that the God of orthodox Christianity has no place in the modern world. Others follow with the assertion that the church is dead. These hold that the church, as we know it today, has outlived its usefulness and has nothing to offer modern man.

This latter idea is accompanied by the theory that God, while He has worked in times past through the church, is not limited to the church for carrying out His plans. God is active in history, they say, and is working to bring a better future for mankind through movements outside the church. The true church is where the action is producing a better future for mankind. Join the revolution!

Such positions create a climate of uncertainty as to the legitimacy of the mission of the church as it has been understood by Christians during past generations. We are told that we must not seek the conversion of individuals now, but rather seek to remake society. Society has sinned against individuals, allowing conditions to exist that condemn the individual to failure and frustration. Therefore society must repent. We must produce a new society where ghettos,

11

poverty, exploitation of the laboring man, and racial discrimination cannot exist.

While such concepts contain praiseworthy objectives, they are inadequate and contrary to biblical teaching as to God's method of redemption. It is not the purpose of this book to defend the orthodox position. At this juncture we simply reaffirm the conviction that the Bible is God's Word to man and must be accepted by Christians as their guide. The church which Jesus established is not destined to disappear from the modern scene, for Jesus said, "The gates of hell shall not prevail against it" (Mt 16:18). Nor is it necessary to defend every organization, attitude, or movement that calls itself Christian. Although much of what is called the church today admittedly has ceased to be relevant to the needs of man, the true church has not been superseded in God's economy. Rather, the visible church often has been something less than the true church of Jesus Christ.

The true church will not only continue to exist, but it has a unique ministry to the world for which no substitute can be found. This is because only the gospel has the power required to transform individuals. There is no hope for a better world except as the men that make up that world become better men. Therefore the divine imperative is to preach the gospel that will transform man's character. This is the primary mission of the church, and this is why we are concerned about church planting. Each true local church is a living cell of the body of Christ. It has within it the power to expand and reproduce itself. This task must continue until Christ's return, when He will gather the wheat into His barn and burn the tares with fire (Mt 13:24-30). The company of the redeemed will then become the nucleus for the kingdom of God to be established upon the earth (Lk 19:17; Mt 19:28; Rev 19:8, 14; 20:6).

Thus church planting is in essence the carrying out of the divine commission, and those who do so do have the promise of Christ that He will be with them "even unto the end of the age" (Mt 28:18-20).

1

The Imperative of Church Planting

THE TRUE CHURCH is the present manifestation of the kingdom of God. As Peter Beyerhaus said, "The Church is, at one and the same time, the community of the redeemed and the redeeming community."[1] The church is God's agent in the earth—the medium through which He expresses Himself to the world. God has no other redeeming agency in the earth.

The church is brought into existence by the preaching of the gospel. Individuals hear the message of Christ proclaimed, calling them to turn from their sins and to believe in Christ as their only Saviour (Ro 10:8-13). The Holy Spirit convinces them of their need so they repent and turn in faith to Christ as Saviour. God forgives their sins, and the Holy Spirit produces a spiritual regeneration so that they are born again by the Spirit (Jn 3:5). Water baptism follows as a visible testimony of the inward change. Such converted people are by the very act of regeneration made members of the body of Christ, which is His church (Gal 3:26-29; 1 Co 12:13).

It follows, therefore, that a person becomes a member of the true church as the result of a spiritual experience. People are not born Christians, even though they may be born into

1. Peter Beyerhaus and Henry Lefever, *The Responsible Church and the Foreign Mission* (Grand Rapids, Mich.: Eerdmans, 1964), p. 110.

15

Christian families. Baptism and church membership make a person a member of a visible Christian community, but there must be an accompanying spiritual experience for the person to be a valid member of the spiritual church—the body of Christ.

The church is a divine organism in an alien environment. The church is in the world, but not of the world (Jn 17:16). For what purpose does God keep the church in the world? What is the church's mission? What should be its activities?

The Bible teaches that the church is in the world to fulfill a three-fold mission.

First, the church is God's own treasure in which He delights. The church's mission is to serve and glorify God, worshiping Him in Spirit and in truth (Eph 1:18; 5:25-27; Ac 13:2; Jn 4:23-24).

Then, the church has a qualitative ministry to itself, building up and perfecting its members, and thus strengthening and edifying the church (Eph 4:11-16; 1 Co 12:1-19; Ro 12:3-16).

Finally, the church has a responsibility to announce the good news of the kingdom to lost men and women, and to be a witness of the power of the gospel (Ac 1:8; Mt 28:18-20; Lk 24:47), thus enlarging the church numerically.

The evangelistic emphasis of the ministry of the church is to be seen in the words of Jesus in the Great Commission: "All power is given unto me in heaven and in earth. Go ye therefore, and teach all nations, baptizing them in the name of the Father, and of the Son, and of the Holy Ghost: teaching them to observe all things whatsoever I have commanded you: and, lo, I am with you alway, even unto the end of the world" (Mt 28:18-20). It is evident that a principal thrust of the church must be evangelistic, reaching out to men and women who have no knowledge of the gospel, bringing them into the kingdom of God. In this way the church exercises its ministry as God's agent for redemption in the world (2 Co 5:18-20). The church thus fulfills its three-fold mission of worshiping God, strengthening itself in the faith, and evangelizing the lost.

The history of the early church as recorded in the book of Acts confirms the importance of the evangelistic emphasis. Immediately after the outpouring of the Holy Spirit on the day of Pentecost, there began a tremendous outreach for the unconverted, resulting in multiplied thousands of converts within the first few months of the life of the church. The church at Jerusalem moved out from its home base to Samaria, Antioch, Damascus, and other cities. The church in Antioch in turn sent out the first missionaries to the Gentiles—Barnabas and Paul—initiating the great missionary program of the early church.

Everywhere that Barnabas and Paul went they preached the gospel, and the resulting converts were brought together in local churches. These local churches in turn continued the work of evangelism and of establishing other churches. As an example of this, we find Paul preaching for two years in Ephesus in Asia Minor (Ac 19:10), and as a result all of Asia heard the Word of the Lord, so that at a later date John could write to the seven churches of Asia. Thus we have the biblical pattern of the early church carrying out its God-given mission.

A study of the New Testament shows that the local church is of utmost importance. The local church is the gathering together of believers in one area for the purpose of worship, self-edification, and to carry on the work of evangelism. Jesus said "Where two or three are gathered together in my name, there am I in the midst of them" (Mt 18:20). The local church is a living cell of the body of Christ, operating in the community where it is located. We should not limit this concept to the meeting of the Christians in a church building. The early church met together in homes, synagogues, public or private dwellings, for worship and edification. But when they were not together in one place, the believers were still the salt of the earth and witnesses for Christ in the society in which they lived.

The local church is an expression of the body of Christ to its community, and God's agent for evangelism in witnessing to the unsaved in that area. It is not enough for an evangelist to raise up a group of converts; it is necessary for the church to be established in order to express the will and purposes of God by fulfilling its mission to the world. The task of evangelism is not complete until local churches are established.

Just as the Holy Spirit possessed and used the Christians in the early church to meet the need of their day, so now the Holy Spirit is able to possess and use Christians to meet the need of our generation.

Let us remember that it is not God's purpose in this stage of history to Christianize the world. The Scripture plainly teaches us that conditions in the world are to get worse as the end approaches (1 Ti 4:1). The purpose of God for our time is to give a witness to the entire world of the gospel of Christ, redeem a people from the world for his name which will be the nucleus of the kingdom of God yet to be established at the return of Christ (Ac 15:14). While He is accomplishing this, He also desires to use that nucleus in the further extension of the church in the earth. The primary mission of the church as it relates to the world, then, is to witness to men everywhere of the gospel of the grace of God and to plant churches which will multiply themselves and extend the witness of their living Lord.

2

The Message That Plants Churches

THE APOSTLE PAUL placed prime importance on the message that he preached. In his writing to the Ephesian church he showed the connection between the message preached and the church that he had founded; "In whom ye also trusted, after that ye heard the word of truth, the gospel of your salvation: in whom also after that ye believed, ye were sealed with the Holy Spirit of promise" (Eph 1:13).

Again, writing to the church in Thessalonica, "For this cause also thank we God without ceasing, because, when ye received the word of God which ye heard of us, ye received it not as the word of men, but as it is in truth, the word of God, which effectually worketh also in you that believe" (1 Th 2:13).

The local church comes into existence as a result of the message preached. The quality of the message determines the quality of the church. The message that builds churches is a Bible-based message. It is in the Scriptures that God's revelation of saving truth is found. Let the church planter be a proclaimer of redemption truth as set forth in the written Word of God, so that the converts may become people of the Book.

All ministers of the Christian church professedly preach

19

the message of the gospel. However, there is a wide variation in the emphasis given. Some of the preaching that goes forth from modern pulpits under the name of the preaching of God's Word has very little resemblance to the message of the apostles. We do not hesitate to affirm that the preaching of the apostolic message in the power of the Spirit will produce a vital apostolic church.

The apostolic message was completely Christ-centered. One has only to read the first sermons of the apostles in the book of Acts to be struck by its straightforward simplicity. At first the message involved little more than the proclamation of the crucifixion and resurrection of Jesus Christ, and that forgiveness of sins and eternal life would be given to those who would believe in Christ. The listeners were exhorted to be baptized, and promised that they would receive the gift of the Spirit (Ac 2:38-39). Though it contained only the barest outlines of Christian theology, yet it contained the essential elements to produce a vital Christian church. Although the apostles, particularly Paul, through the inspiration of the Spirit, later developed and rounded out the theology of the Christian church, and explained more fully the purposes of God, yet the message remained completely Christ-centered.

The message that plants churches today must likewise be Christ-centered. A great part of the message of the gospel consists in explaining who Jesus Christ is, what He did on earth, the significance of His death and resurrection, what He is doing and willing to do for those who believe in Him now; and His future triumph in the universe. The good news that redeems man and forms churches is to be found in these basic truths of the gospel.

Christ Jesus brings us back into proper relationship with the universe in which we live. He makes us at peace with

God and with ourselves. Sin has disjointed man from his proper relationships. Christ Jesus came to remedy this.

The planter of churches will avoid too great an emphasis on negative preaching in his message. However, some negative preaching is necessary. The sinner must hear the thunderings of God's righteous law against his sin in order to be awakened to his need of a Saviour. Idolatrous practices must be challenged in the name of the true God. Through the power of the Holy Spirit, the tragedy of a sinful life must be revealed, but all of this is only preliminary to pointing to the one true Saviour.

Let us be careful not to give the impression that being a Christian consists in not doing certain things. The fact that a person does not drink, smoke, dance, or gamble does not make him a Christian, nor do the clothes, jewelry, or makeup that he or she does or does not wear. Only faith in the living Christ can save. This fact must be kept ever preeminent.

The evangelist should not simply attack the priests or witch doctors of the prevailing religion. Let his message present the living gospel, backed up by the power of God. Let him preach deliverance from fear and bondage. Let him proclaim Christ as the great Deliverer, the loving Saviour, and the powerful Redeemer.

Evangelists must take care not to try to advance on too broad a front. The introduction of political issues into the message will only serve to weaken the fine cutting edge of the gospel. We do not deny that Christianity has implications that reach every phase of life—both individual and national—but when we are planting churches, we are not dealing with national issues and injustices. We are dealing with the individual and his need as a sinful, rebellious soul—the prodigal who needs to return to the house of his father. Let us take care not to introduce secondary matters that weaken the impact of the gospel on the individual life and relieve him of his responsibility as an individual who must stand before the great Judge of all the earth.

The message that the church planter preaches must be relevant to the needs of his hearers. The gospel must be presented in such a way that it will show how the specific needs of individuals can be met. In cultures of certain religious backgrounds, there is an overwhelming sense of moral guilt. The evangelist can proclaim to such people the unique message of forgiveness through the cross of Christ. In other cultures, the sense of guilt because of moral failure or sin may be very weak, or almost nonexistent. There may, however, exist an overwhelming fear of evil spirits which affects every area of life. In this case, the people are likely to respond to the wonderful, comforting truth that Jesus is Lord of all, and that when He commanded the spirits they obeyed Him. It can be shown that the Holy Spirit is more powerful than any of the evil spirits in the world (1 Jn 4:4). Thus, their need is met on a different level, but it is very definitely met by the provisions of the gospel.

It is perhaps a universal experience of man that he feels alone in the world. Every man feels the need of help from beyond himself. Some religions cultivate ancestral worship in the hope of bringing communion, fellowship, and protection from the spirit world. The human heart was made for fellowship with God, and every life has the capacity to respond to the unique friendship of the Son of God.

Neither Jesus nor the apostles ignored the physical need of men in ministering to them. True, Christ used the opportunity to explain the deeper needs of the soul, but he healed both the physically and spiritually afflicted (Mk 2:5-12). One evangelist of my acquaintance has brought thousands to Christ and raised up dozens of churches. He does not claim to be a healer. He simply preaches the gospel of Christ and tells how Jesus healed the sick when He was on earth, and proclaims to his hearers that Jesus is the same today and will hear their prayers if they call to Him in faith.

A constant and growing need in the heart of men is the need for hope. Man wants something to live for in this life and a hope beyond the grave. What a message we have when we can present a resurrected Christ who imparts eternal life now, and gives us promise of life beyond the present world! Certainly, this is the message that appeals to a universal need.

It is important that the supernatural element in the gospel be presented to the people. The message of Christianity is not simply a code of ethics or a philosophy of life. The gospel is about a Person who died and rose again. The gospel presents the exciting prospects of divine intervention in the lives of ordinary men. This usually occurs first in conversion.

The preacher of the gospel should not look upon conversion as merely a psychological phenomenon, but as the direct intervention of God in the life of an individual. It is called "being born again" (Jn 3:5-8). It is the coming of the life of Christ to us. The gospel teaches that God is interested in man as an individual. He is not simply the God of history, nor the impersonal God of a life force. He is a personal God who wants to be a Father to man; a God who has made provision for man's spiritual, psychological, and physical needs; a God who will step in, in the course of human existence, and change both the people and their circumstances. God imparts a new life, God answers the prayer of His children, God supplies material needs, God heals our sick bodies. Man is not dependent simply on his own mental and physical resources, but can receive help from beyond himself.

In preaching the gospel, the evangelist must be careful to show man's responsibility to God. It is not enough to preach simply the benefits of the gospel—how that Christ delivers from sin, gives a person peace and happiness, breaks the chains of evil habits, and gives us hope of eternal life. We must also show that Christ is not only Saviour, but Lord. Jesus told time and time again that in order to follow Christ we must be willing to leave all. In Luke 14:25-35 He tells the great multitude that followed Him, that they must be willing to leave father, mother, wife, children, and brethren for His sake. They should be willing to forsake all that they have. They should not place the preservation of their own lives above obedience to Him. The message of the gospel not only indicates that man can receive benefits in Christ Jesus, but also that God requires an absolute and complete surrender to the lordship of Christ.

Let us then preach a Christ-centered message, proclaiming all of the marvelous benefits that may be received, and aiming our message at the felt need of the hearers. At the same time, let us not neglect to insist on total commitment as a requisite of discipleship, so that the converts will be sold out to God, men who will follow the footsteps of the apostles. In so doing, we shall lay a solid foundation for the church and for its expansion in our corner of the earth.

3

The Holy Spirit–the Power for Church Planting

THE HOLY SPIRIT is the divine dynamic working in the world through the agency of the church for the redemption of man. In the beginning, when God created the world, we are told that the Spirit moved upon the face of the waters (Gen 1:2), so that order was produced from chaos. Likewise, God has now planned a new creation in Christ Jesus. His purpose is to redeem man from the chaos of sin. The Holy Spirit moves upon lost humanity, causing the glorious light of the gospel to penetrate the darkness.

In order to bring about the creation of this new humanity which God creates in Christ Jesus, the Holy Spirit does the following:

1. He works with the proclaimer of gospel truth, enduing him with wisdom and power (Ac 1:8), thus convicting men of sin, righteousness and judgment. (Jn 16:8; Ac 2:37-38).

2. He continually points men to Christ as the only Saviour. He leads the awakened sinner to the cross where Jesus was crucified for his sin. The Holy Spirit interprets to him the meaning of the resurrection. As the sinner responds in faith, he is saved from sin and hell by the working of regeneration by the Spirit. A new life is imparted to him, so that he is

born again (Titus 3:5; Ro 4:24-25; Jn 3:5). By this new birth the believer becomes a part of the church—a member of the body of Christ (Eph 2:17-22).

3. The Holy Spirit comes to the believer to dwell in His temple. This in the Scriptures is called the gift of the Holy Spirit (Ac 1:5; 2:38), or the baptism with the Holy Spirit (Lk 3:16; Ac 11:16). It is also referred to as "the promise of the Father" (Lk 24:49).

4. He perfects the Christian in holiness. His inward ministry in the character of the believer results in the fruit of the Spirit being manifested in the believer's life (Gal 5:22-26).

5. As a member of the body of Christ, each believer has a potential for spiritual ministry. The Holy Spirit distributes gifts to the believers, "severally as He will" so that each Christian may be used by God for the edifying of the church and winning the lost to Christ (1 Co 12:1-13).

In our approach to church planting, then, we must realize that the work is God's. The whole plan of redemption, the conversion of the lost, and the founding of the church was in the mind of God before the world began (Lk 24:46-47; Mt 16:18). It is a high privilege to be a co-laborer with God in this divine work of redeeming man.

Our part is to follow the divine initiative. To bring this about, believers must be filled with and controlled by the Spirit. Care must be taken to give heed to divine guidance. Philip was so directed when he left a spiritual awakening in the city of Samaria to go and talk to a man in the desert (Ac 8:26). There must be a continuous submission to the divine will. The apostle Peter probably had no plan to go to the Gentiles, but he lived close enough to God so that the Holy Spirit could speak to him and direct him into a new course of action. Thus the house of Cornelius heard the Word of the Lord, and the door of faith was open to the Gentiles (Ac

10). Cultivation of this spiritual sensitivity is of utmost importance to the planter of churches.

The activity of the Holy Spirit is not confined to the evangelist or the church planter. The whole church is the temple for the dwelling of God by the Spirit (1 Co 6:19-20). The Spirit desires to dwell in the whole church and to direct all of its members, and not the minister only. For this reason *all* were filled with the Spirit on the day of Pentecost and not just the apostles. The whole church is the body of Christ, the instrumentality that the Holy Spirit uses to exalt Christ and to draw the unconverted to Him.

It is therefore urgent that pastors and evangelists preach and teach the necessity for all believers to be filled with the Spirit (Eph 5:18-19). We must also encourage these believers to be sensitive to the guidance of the Spirit and to offer themselves to God as instruments of blessing so that they will become useful members of the body of Christ. Further, we should teach the church that all Christians are to seek to ascertain their particular ministry as a member of the body of Christ, and thus contribute to the adding up of the church (1 Co 12:1-13). The Holy Spirit imparts the enabling necessary to make effective that ministry.

Of great importance is the spiritual development of believers in Christian character so that they manifest the fruit of holiness and love. Paul teaches us that although believers may give an inspired utterance or have faith to move mountains, or attain great spiritual knowledge, yet, without the fruit of love, their achievements become of no value to them (1 Co 13). Christ Himself said, "By their fruits ye shall know them" (Mt 7:20). The development of the fruit of the Spirit is a paramount ministry of the Spirit (Gal 5:22-25).

4

The Church Planter

THE CHURCH PLANTER may be a missionary, an evangelist, pastor, or a layman, who, in the providence of God, has been given the opportunity to establish a church. The objective will be to present Christ to the community, to win converts, and then to incorporate these converts into a local church.

What kind of person should the church planter be? God sometimes passes by the most likely person who from a human viewpoint would be most qualified to do the work and uses unlikely instruments. In outlining the qualifications of a church planter, there is no desire to eliminate anyone who has been, or can be, used of God for this work, but rather, simply to outline those qualifications which would normally be expected of a person in this capacity, and which might serve also as a goal to those individuals who are being used in this ministry.

Let us first examine the *natural* qualifications. The church planter should be socially and educationally acceptable to the people that he seeks to reach. While there are many exceptions to this rule, men with a rural background have more success in rural communities, while the urban population probably will not respond as well to the man from a rural cultural environment. Educated people are more likely to be receptive to a man whose education is comparable to their own.

Then, because the very nature of church planting requires that the church planter deal with new people, he should have an outgoing personality, be able to meet new people easily, and engage in conversation about spiritual things with all classes of people.

It is not often that an introverted personality, one who tends to isolate himself and be uncomfortable in the presence of people, particularly strangers, will be a successful church planter. However, once again, this rule has its exceptions, for we have known persons who do not make friends easily and are not adept at carrying on conversation with strangers, who have been able to plant churches. Their lack, however, is usually compensated by other factors that attract the people to the message they preach, even though interpersonal communication is difficult. Such men are sometimes men of prayer, with a special anointing in their ministry, and have such outstanding results in answer to prayer that people are attracted and a church established.

The church planter must be sincerely interested in people and have a deep concern for their personal problems. He must have ability to apply spiritual truths for their solution. He must be willing to give time and energy to help others. He should constantly trust God to give him the needed insight into the problems of the people and manifest his deep concern for them (1 Th 2:5-9).

Such characteristics as ability in public speaking, an attractive personality, and an exemplary family life will place the minister in a better position to win his hearers to Christ.

As to *spiritual* qualifications, he must be, first of all, a man of God. This means that he will have had contact with God in the changing circumstances of his own life. He will have had a spiritual rebirth. He should have a well-developed, mature Christian character with his speech and habits exemplifying the virtues of the gospel. He should be a man who is filled with the Spirit of God.

The church planter must be motivated by a deep and abiding compassion for the lost. He must be moved by the sacrificial devotion that impelled the shepherd to leave the comforts of the fold to go into the night and seek the lost sheep (Lk 15:3-7). He must seek the lost with the patient persistence of the woman who diligently swept the whole house in order to find a lost coin (Lk 15:8-10). And like the father of the prodigal, he will never give up until he sees his wayward son returning home (Lk 15:11-32).

The church planter will be man of prayer. The apostle Paul is an inspiring example of this important ministry (Col 1:9-11; 2:1-3; Eph 3:14-19). To the Thessalonians he wrote: "We give thanks to God always for you all, making mention of you in our prayers; remembering without ceasing your work of faith, and labor of love, and patience of hope . . . in the sight of God and our Father" (1 Th 1:2-3). Note also the command of Christ in relationship to meeting the need of lost men. "Pray ye therefore the Lord of the harvest, that he will send laborers into his harvest" (Mt 9:38).

Normally, we would consider that he would be one who has dedicated his life to the work of the ministry. There are cases, of course, where a church has come into existence through the efforts of a lay Christian who has evidenced his concern for others by witnessing to friends and neighbors. This is by no means a rarity. Even so, the Christian layman who has been responsible for the gathering together of a group must usually seek the help of more experienced ministers in establishing this new church on solid foundations.

The church planter will be a man of vision. He will see

possibilities where others only see obstacles. He will be highly motivated and persevere in spite of discouraging setbacks. His vision is backed up by a solid faith that God has sent him to do this work and will see him through.

Most churches are established because of the vision, spiritual burden, sacrifice, and perseverance of some individual who gave himself to the task of church planting. I well remember one pastor who was developing an outstation several miles from the main church. He not only encouraged lay workers to visit the place, but he himself often made the trip of several miles on foot to minister there. He told of how the rain would sometimes catch him on the road. The hills were so steep and slippery that he would have to climb them on hands and knees. He said that he sometimes reached his home at 2:30 A.M. covered with mud from head to foot. He had no financial need to do this. His church was taking care of him very well. But he was impelled by his love for the work. Shortly after that conversation, he informed me that the church had been organized with one of his own lay workers as pastor, and now he no longer found it necessary to make the trip. This is the spirit that plants churches!

5

The Process of Church Planting

THERE IS NO SINGLE METHOD for raising up churches. Under the guidance of the Holy Spirit, one method may succeed where other methods have failed. The choice of method will depend on many factors not the least of which will be the qualities of the worker and his approach to the task. If the evangelist who is to start the work is to remain as the pastor until the church is well established, this will influence the approach. If he is to hold a campaign and expect someone else to become the pastor of the church, then other provisions must be made.

An evangelist or missionary who holds a campaign in a new place where there is no established church to take care of the converts must include in his plan the care of the converts which result from his evangelistic effort. It is a grave error, if not a sin, to bring a group of converts into existence and then leave them without proper care. Some evangelists feel that their task is limited to preaching and winning the multitudes. Sometimes they have success in winning scores and perhaps hundreds of new converts, but when the campaign is over, they feel they have discharged their obligation and move into other places without having made provision for the new converts which they have left behind. This is often

32

the signal for false teachers to move and carry away the converts. Also, many who have been truly awakened and converted without spiritual help become discouraged. Many lose out completely and others fail to grow. Not only are the results of the campaign largely lost, but the next evangelist will find it more difficult to come in and do a permanent work.

Where a missionary or an evangelist expects to hold a campaign in a new place, he must think ahead and see how to provide for the new converts. There are perhaps three alternatives. First, the evangelist who is raising up the church may himself stay on and become the permanent pastor; second, the evangelist may bring a co-worker with him who will plan to stay on after the evangelist is gone. This man will work with him during the campaign in the instruction of new converts and then stay on as pastor. Third, the evangelist or missionary, while not planning to stay on as pastor, may nevertheless stay long enough to develop local leadership to take the oversight of the new congregation. This last was the apostle Paul's method.

Another problem that must be solved is the matter of a meeting place for the new congregation. Properties in the larger cities especially are expensive and often beyond the reach of the new congregation. It would be a mistake to make an outright gift of a building to a new congregation even when this is possible. The members of the congregation must feel that the church is their church, and therefore they must assume some responsibility for their building. Probably in the present-day system of evangelism, we have made the matter of church buildings more important than it really should be. In New Testament times this problem evidently did not assume major proportions. Nevertheless, given our modern circumstances, the acquiring of a meeting place is a problem that must be resolved. Some countries have govern-

ment restrictions that limit the meeting of persons for religious services to specific locations dedicated to this purpose.
In such cases, the matter of a proper place for meeting goes
hand in hand with the establishing of a church. Even so, in
the initial stages of church planting, the acquiring of a permanent building should be considered as of secondary importance, priority being given to the spiritual aspects of winning the lost to Christ. Many times, once the Spirit of God
begins to move, the question of housing for the congregation
may be solved in what may appear to be an almost miraculous
manner. When the greater spiritual need is met, the material
aspect is more readily resolved.

There are several different ways to initiate a campaign.
The evangelist may hold an open-air campaign on a piece of
ground which he has leased for a few months or a year. He
might pitch a tent, erect a temporary structure, or simply
build a platform and set up lights and a public address system. As the number of converts grows, offerings can be taken
up for the purchasing of a permanent site and the erection
of a simple building. Sometimes a building such as a theater
or warehouse can be rented with the congregation paying
the rent; or if the down payment is made, the new church
can pick up the monthly payments.

Another plan may be followed in areas where a church is
to be established in a new city, but where other churches
already exist in the country, thus providing a source of
workers. As the evangelistic campaign comes to a close, instead of trying to secure a building suitable for a large congregation, the converts may be divided up into small groups
in the different sectors of the city. Bible school students or
pastors with experience can be placed in charge of these
groups which meet in rented houses or buildings. The leaders
work with the group so that each will grow sufficiently to be-

come an established church and eventually meet its own building needs.

This has been successful in more than one of the Central American capitals. In an evangelistic meeting in San Salvador which brought in over 350 baptized converts, the converts and interested friends were divided up into twelve groups throughout the city. Workers from neighboring churches and from the Bible school were pressed into service. In one year there were twelve established churches in the city, which in the course of the next ten years grew to about forty in the city and its environs. This method, of course, depends upon the availability of potential pastors who can be given the responsibility for these new groups.

A word may be said in favor of this latter method. It does not make as impressive a picture for a thousand Christians to be scattered among twenty churches throughout a city instead of them all being housed under one roof; yet, without question there are many advantages. For one thing, in the beginning stages of the establishing of a church in a country it is most difficult to find a pastor of sufficient capacity to care for a church of 500 converts. It is not nearly so difficult to find workers who can take care of a group of fifty. Further, by scattering them out through the city, probably they are actually reaching a larger section of the population than would be the case were all the activities centered in one location.

6

The Process of Church Planting (Cont.)

LET US NOW STUDY the steps to be taken to establish a church in a new area, opening with an evangelistic campaign. There are three main steps: The preparation for the campaign, the campaign itself, and the follow-up.

PREPARATION FOR THE CAMPAIGN

Church planting is basically a spiritual task which must be accomplished by spiritual means. Therefore spiritual preparation is exceedingly important. If there are already Christians in the area, they should be encouraged to participate in a prayer effort to prepare the ground for the sowing of the seed. If there are no Christians in the area, then the evangelist and his fellow workers must carry the main burden of preparing the ground spiritually. If there are churches in nearby towns, it will be of great benefit to secure the prayer support of spiritual people in these churches.

A group of Christians who will give themselves to earnest prayer for the success of the campaign can be used of God to produce a receptive climate, defeating the powers of darkness that oppose any forward move for the kingdom of God. We cannot overestimate the effectiveness of such prayer warriors. Many outstanding evangelists state that they owe

36

their success to the faithful prayers of men and women who secretly wage spiritual warfare on their behalf. Paul describes the importance of this ministry in his description of the Christian soldier. He declares that our warfare is not against flesh and blood, but against spiritual powers that rule the darkness of this world. He finalizes the passage with a request that such prayer warfare may be directed toward the success of his own ministry. "Praying always . . . for me, that utterance may be given me, that I may open my mouth boldly to make known the mystery of the gospel" (Eph 6:10-19).

Location of the Evangelism Effort

The matter of where to begin is important. Circumstances may be the determining factor. Even so, a few guidelines may be helpful.

Go where the people are! As a general rule, the population centers should be chosen in preference to the sparsely settled areas. Many a church has not prospered because it was too far removed from the center of population. The fact that a lot may have been donated for the purpose of building a church is not sufficient reason to locate the building at the edge of town. The securing of a location in the heart of the business district may not be as great an advantage as would appear at first glance, since the people may live too far away. The new effort should be located where it will be easily accessible by roads, trains, or buses, so that the greatest response may be obtained.

Probably the plans for a permanent location for the emerging church should not be made at the very beginning of the effort. There are advantages in waiting until the response can be evaluated. Several campaigns held in different sections of the city may point up the area of the greatest response. Also it could well result that instead of establishing one church, three or four churches may develop from the effort. Securing of a permanent building is not in the first order of importance. What really counts is to find the best way of reaching the most people for Christ. The use of a lot for open-air services, a rented theater building, or a sports area will provide the opportunity to bring the witness to various sections of the city and give the Holy Spirit the chance to direct before putting down stakes too deeply. Flexibility is important to evangelism.

There should be house-to-house *visitation* in preparation for the evangelistic effort. If the evangelist can secure a group of Christian workers, they should engage in daily visitation, visiting all of the houses in the area, giving out gospel literature, speaking to the residents about their spiritual needs, and inviting them to the campaign. In fact, even if there is to be no evangelistic campaign with an outside evangelist, the church planter may well follow this method in order to get a hearing in the community. In some efforts of this nature, thousands of homes are visited. It is almost impossible to have contact with this number of people without finding responsive hearts.

Announcements of the meetings should be made. The methods employed will depend upon the local facilities. Posters can be placed in prominent places, and handbills distributed. One-minute spot announcements on the radio are very effective. Some evangelists have secured the services of television to interest people in the campaign. Probably, one- to five-minute presentations over the television or radio are the best in the preparatory stage of the campaign. Announcements can be made in local newspapers, and a sound truck may be employed to announce the meetings.

THE EVANGELISTIC CAMPAIGN

If a campaign of evangelism is envisioned, the following guidelines should prove helpful:

1. The evangelist and his fellow workers should come to the meetings having spent time in prayer and spiritual preparation, expecting God to manifest Himself.

2. Let the message be Biblical and simple, with emphasis on the fact that God hears and answers prayer, conveying to the listeners the reality of the Christian message.

3. Keep the services lively and moving. The singing should be inspirational with plenty of choruses in order to maintain the interest of the casual visitor. Testimonies of people who have found deliverance from sin or healing in answer to prayer will keep the attention of the listeners and awaken them to an attitude of faith.

4. There should be a chance for people to accept Christ in every service.

5. Those making a profession of faith should be visited in their homes.

CONSERVING THE RESULTS

It is of utmost importance that teaching be given to the new converts while the campaign is still in full swing. The evangelist or the person who is to remain as pastor of the new church should arrange a time every afternoon or evening so new converts may receive special instruction in preparation for baptism. This has been done with good results employing the half hour before the regular evening services. It is too late to wait until the enthusiasm of the campaign is over to begin to teach the converts. They should be encouraged to enter classes for new converts on the day they make their first step toward Christ.[1]

1. See chap. 7, "The Care of New Converts."

Home study courses are available that will be helpful in establishing new converts. Usually, these come in series of lessons and give the fundamentals of the gospel. These can be given out to the new converts, who are instructed to study them in their homes and send their answers to the proper person for corrections and additional help. When unconverted people take the course, by the time the course is finished, they may be ready to make a public confession of Christ as their Saviour and enter the new converts' class.[2]

An evangelistic campaign of this nature should not be too short in duration. A campaign could very well run from three to six months. By continuing a campaign nightly over a long period of time, the new converts have a chance to become accustomed to their new life and established in their faith. For people who have come from non-Christian or nonevangelical background this long period of contact with the simple message of the gospel helps them to make the transition. Campaigns of two or three weeks duration may have great results in numbers, but often the greater number of people fail to become members of the church. However, when a campaign continues for three months or longer, there is much more hope of achieving a greater percentage of permanent results.

The evangelist should not be surprised if the same people respond to the invitation night after night. God knows when the light breaks through and a full assurance of salvation comes to the individual. In the meantime, they should be encouraged to seek God. Also their continued response gives the evangelist and workers the opportunity to deal with each

2. The Light of Life series, Christian Literature, Inc., Box 718, Santa Ana, Calif.; *The Great Questions of Life*, International Correspondence Institute, 1445 Boonville Ave., Springfield, Mo., 65802; and *The Good News* course (in several languages), Moody Correspondence School, 820 N. LaSalle St., Chicago, Ill., 60610.

one individually. This is especially important in the large campaigns where the amount of visitation in the homes is necessarily limited because of the many people who respond to the invitation.

7

The Care of New Converts

WHEN JESUS RENEWED Peter's commission after his tragic failure, he told him to "feed my lambs" (Jn 21:15). We are told
in some parts of the world less than one half of the infants
born reach their first birthday. Likewise, there is no question
but that the church suffers its greatest loss by its failure to
hold new converts until they mature. What a congregation
most churches would have if all of the people who accepted
Christ were still with them today! It is true that the Scripture says that some of the seed will be lost on the wayside and
some fall among thorns, but there is a widespread conviction
that we are losing more converts than we should.

CARE AT TIME OF CONVERSION

Healthy children are normally healthy at birth. A child
that is not born with good health may be weak and sickly all
his life. It is necessary for us as Christian workers to do
everything we can to see that those who accept the Lord
either in campaigns or in our churches have a healthy birth
into the kingdom of God.

The first step is to provide for special care at the hour of
conversion. The evangelist should prepare a group of personal workers to deal with those that accept Christ as their

Saviour. These workers should be given more than superficial instruction. They should be people of true spiritual experience, that understand the Scripture, and have a deep desire to see souls born into the kingdom of God. Many times we have been disappointed with the help that is offered to those who come forward to accept Christ as their Saviour. Sometimes this help is no more than taking the name of the individual and his address, purportedly to follow up the profession of faith by a contact in the home. Too often this is not carried out. We must do our best to see that the person who accepts Christ experiences a true spiritual conversion. Something more than an evangelical ritualism is required. The decision must be based upon a true faith and the will of the convert must be involved so that it becomes something more than an emotional experience. It is necesary that the faith of the convert be based on the Word of God. The worker may read to him one of the many promises that give hope and a basis of faith for the new convert, and help the inquirer to understand these passages as a basis of faith.

It will help when leading a seeker to Christ to point out definite steps that the seeker must take. The following steps are based on the Word of God. The Scripture texts should be read to the seeker or by him aloud.

1. *Place the attention on the Lord Jesus Christ.* The sinner must look away from himself, his inadequacies, and his sins and see that there is a Saviour, who can help him. "Believe on the Lord Jesus Christ, and thou shalt be saved, and thy house" (Ac 16:31).

2. *Confess sins to receive forgiveness.* "If we confess our sins, he is faithful and just to forgive us our sins, and to cleanse us from all unrighteousness" (1 Jn 1:9).

3. *Turn from sin to God.* "Repent, and be baptized every one of you in the name of Jesus Christ for the remission of

sins, and ye shall receive the gift of the Holy Ghost" (Ac 2:38).

4. *Receive Christ by an act of faith.* "As many as received him, to them gave he power to become the sons of God, even to them that believe on his name: which were born, not of blood, nor of the will of the flesh, nor of the will of man, but of God" (Jn 1:12-13).

"If thou shalt confess with thy mouth the Lord Jesus, and shalt believe in thine heart that God hath raised him from the dead, thou shalt be saved. For with the heart man believeth unto righteousness; and with the mouth confession is made unto salvation. For the scripture saith, Whosoever believeth on him shall not be ashamed" (Ro 10:9-11).

The penitent should be encouraged to pray to God in his own words and confess his sins. It is necessary that he, himself, have a vital contact with God. We should not consider that our duty toward the convert is discharged by telling him that he has accepted Christ and now is a Christian. Many have come forward in a sort of evangelical ritual, without achieving any real contact with Christ, which, of course results in disillusionment. We need to be willing to spend time with these converts. One or two minutes may not be enough. The worker should encourage the convert to call upon the Lord, keeping in mind the promises of salvation, until the Spirit of God has an opportunity to break through the spiritual darkness and give a revelation of Christ to his soul.

5. *Tell others about Christ.* "Whosoever shall confess me before men, him shall the Son of man also confess before the angels of God" (Lk 12:8).

"Ye shall be witnesses unto me" (Ac 1:8).

Spiritual Sponsors

Some churches have had good success in establishing a

program of spiritual sponsors for new converts. This is done by assigning a spiritual counselor to each new convert to serve as a sort of elder brother and help him in the first few days after his conversion.

The spiritual sponsor should be assigned at the time the convert accepts Christ. He should be a person of good character and ideals and should have a personality and background compatible with that of the new convert. The responsibilities of the sponsor would be:

1. To establish contact with the new convert at the hour of conversion.

2. To visit the convert in his home within a day or two after he has accepted Christ.

3. To accompany him to the next meeting and sit beside him.

4. To pray with him after the service either in the prayer room or at the altar if opportunity is provided.

5. To give him the counsel and help that he needs as far as he is able.

6. To inform the pastor if the new convert encounters difficulties in his spiritual life.

7. To encourage the new convert to enroll in the new convert's class.

8. To help the new convert with the lessons of a home study course and explain their spiritual significance to him.[1]

CLASSES FOR NEW CONVERTS

Just as newborn babes require special care, so new converts require special help and instruction (1 Pe 2:2). Every church should have a special class to give basic instruction to the new converts to prepare them for water baptism and church membership. If there are no converts for a new convert's

1. See fn. 2, p. 40.

class, then the church should seek God for a revival and take definite steps to intensify its evangelistic outreach.

A class for new converts should be held at least once a week. It may be held as a special class in the Sunday school, or a special night of the week might be devoted to it. In evangelistic campaigns where there are many new believers, it is well to begin this class before the campaign ends. Otherwise it will be difficult to conserve the results of the campaign after the evangelist has gone. A successful plan has been to offer the class every night one half hour before the regular service begins.

The teaching should be basic and simple. Whenever possible the pastor should be the one who teaches the new convert's class, since he is the best able to guide them in their first steps with the Lord.[2]

BAPTISM

Baptism is an important step for the new convert. Every care should be taken to prepare him so that it will be a meaningful spiritual experience for him. Baptism should occur as early in the Christian life as is possible. It is a mistake to allow months or years to go by without the convert taking this important step. Such circumstances may exist where the church has failed to give sufficient emphasis or provide opportunity for water baptism. Or the convert may be unwilling to take the step because he feels that he is not yet prepared. Such a circumstance calls for individual help and counsel on the part of the pastor to help the convert resolve his problems. Some teaching is necessary to prepare a convert for baptism. He must be able to understand what he is doing and to as-

2. In our [Assemblies of God] churches in Latin America, the pastors use a Standard of Faith and Fellowship as a guide for teaching these classes. See Appendix C of *The Indigenous Church*, pp. 141-57, for a copy of this standard.

sume the responsibilities of the Christian life. Many pastors do not baptize converts unless they are prepared to become members of the local church. In fact, the very act of baptism is considered the initial step into full membership of the local church. They see no point in baptizing people who are not going to become a part of some local church, or accept the responsibilities of church membership.

The period of teaching also serves another purpose. Particularly in Latin America, many of the people come to the Lord with complications in their marital status. It is not uncommon for couples to live together in common-law marriage. Baptism is considered not only an answer of a clear conscience before God, but also a testimony to the world of a new life in Christ. Therefore, it is believed that new converts should give evidence of their conversion by taking steps to straighten up their lives. The workers should avoid an ultralegalistic approach in this matter, as sin has certainly wrought its havoc, and we cannot always attain the ideal condition that God intended for the Christian home. Nevertheless, every effort should be made to rectify unwholesome conditions and produce fruits "meet for repentance" (Mt 3:8).

Importance should be given to the act of baptism. Friends of the convert should be invited, and the convert should be given an opportunity to confess publicly his faith in Christ.

ACTIVITIES OF THE NEW CONVERTS

It is a mistake to suppose that a new convert must only sit and listen to others. He should begin his Christian life as an active witness. First of all, he should testify to his own family and friends. In fact, when a person accepts Christ, every effort should be made on the part of the workers to see that the whole family comes to Christ. The New Testament has much to say about family conversion. A new convert opens a door to the evangelization of his family.

If the church is active in witnessing to Christ in street services, the new convert should go along and be given the opportunity to tell what Christ has done for him. He should be encouraged also to visit outstations and branch Sunday schools. Of course, he should attend Sunday school and the meetings of the church faithfully.

In the Great Commission, Jesus said that we should "make disciples" (Mt 28:19 NASB). It is one thing to be a believer; it is another thing to be the Lord's disciple. A disciple is a follower and a learner.

Jesus set forth the price of discipleship in several places in the Scripture. In Luke 14:26 He tells us that the disciple must place Christ and His will before his parents, wife, and children, and even above self-preservation! Verse 33 tells us that all of our worldly goods must be placed on the altar. We must be willing to forsake all to follow Christ.

To be a disciple of Christ is to acknowledge His lordship. In salvation we take Christ as our Saviour and rejoice in the knowledge of sins forgiven. However, the price of our salvation is a purchase price. We are not our own; we are bought with a price (1 Co 6:19-20). A disciple acknowledges his Lord's ownership. Paul says that, whether we live or die, we are the Lord's (Ro 14:8).

Actually, Christ's authority over His disciple is totalitarian. He demands all and promises all, for He says that, if we will seek first the kingdom of God and His righteousness, all other things will be given to us (Mt 6:33).

The disciple must learn that every phase of his life—his schooling, business, family, and self—must be brought under the control of Jesus Christ. This is discipleship. This is what makes dynamic Christians and dynamic churches. Let us not be satisfied in leading converts to a superficial concept of what the gospel is.

Spiritual growth is of great importance. The new convert should be taught how to overcome failure. The Spirit-filled life should be shown to him as a practical experience and the ideal for all Christians. The apostle Peter recommends that the convert be sure that his faith be accompanied by virtue (moral excellence), knowledge, temperance, (self-control), patience, godliness (piety), brotherly kindness, and love. If we do these things, he assures us that we shall never fall (2 Pe 1:5-10).

8

Establishing the Church

AFTER THERE ARE CONVERTS or prospective members either as
the result of a campaign or because there are Christians who
already live in the locality, the next step is to form the believers into a local church. The strength of the local church
is its membership. Stable, faithful, instructed members normally produce an active, faithful, growing congregation. In
the previous chapter we dealt with the importance of preparing converts for membership. This preparation includes
teaching the fundamentals of the Christian faith, for a faithful membership must be an instructed membership. It is also
of great importance that the members manifest a true Christian character. Many have an intellectual concept of Christian truth but in actual life do not manifest the fruit of true
conversion. A true Christian is such because of the presence
of vital spiritual life. The work of the church is carried forward not simply by good men, or even instructed men, but by
men who have had contact with God—men who are filled
with the Holy Spirit.

It is important that the church planter be deliberate about
the acceptance of members into the fellowship of the church.
With the first converts he establishes the pattern which will
be followed by the church in years to come. If he allows

50

people to be received into membership who do not have a good testimony in the Christian life, who are not committed to God, and who are indifferent in regard to their Christian responsibilities, he will set the pattern for failure in the future years of the church. Also in his anxiety to enlarge the membership roll, or to get financial or moral backing for his church project, the worker should be careful about receiving those who profess to be Christians but may come to him from other groups with doctrines contrary to those which he preaches. For example, the church planter's objective is to establish a self-supporting congregation. If he takes into membership those who have no sense of responsibility in this area, or who do not believe in tithing, they will not only fail to support the work themselves but discourage others from participating in the support of the work. Another point where care should be exercised is with groups that have split off from another congregation and desire to affiliate with the new church. Sometimes these are contentious people who have left their original congregation because they could not have their own way. Such members will likely cause problems later on, and their presence may be more damaging than beneficial to the new church. The number of members is not as important as their loyalty and stability.

Since the stability of the church depends upon the character, faithfulness, and activity of the members, the first task in organizing the church is to determine which people meet the requirements of membership. A list of members is basic to the organization of the church.

If the church is being established in an entirely new area, then the evangelist or pastor will have given the necessary instruction and examined the converts one by one in anticipation of baptism. Those members who qualify for baptism should be accepted as members of the church. Applicants who have come from other churches or evangelical groups should be examined, too, since to fail to do so may introduce a weak or divisive element into the new church.

It would be wise for the worker to form an examining committee of the most mature Christians to consult with them about the candidates for membership. In this way, the members begin to share in the responsibility in the operation of the church from its inception.

Once there is a list of members, the next step is to confirm the worker who is to serve as pastor by obtaining the approval of the body of believers. In the beginning this might seem to be an almost unnecessary procedure, since the new congregation will normally accept the worker they know, or the worker who is suggested to them without question. However, we are teaching the new congregation the responsibilities which they must bear in the future, and it is preferable to introduce correct practices right from the beginning rather than to effect changes later on.

If the new church is formed as a result of the growth of an outstation of a mother church, the pastor of the mother church, together with the official board will counsel the worker in the development of the new church. The candidates for baptism will be examined by the board of the mother church in the usual way, until the new group is formed into an autonomous church. If a national organization exists, the matter of the time in which the group can achieve autonomy will be decided in consultation among the local worker, the pastor of the mother church, and the officers of the national organization.

After choosing its pastor, the church is now ready to elect its official board. Usually from three to seven deacons are chosen. For a small church, the smaller number is preferable, particularly as it is unlikely that there will be sufficient mature men to fill the posts. If all the members of the congregation are new converts, it would be better to appoint an advisory committee and have the members ratified by the congregation, rather than to choose deacons at the start. This advisory committee could work with the pastor for a year and become acquainted with the organization and management of church business. Perhaps by the second year it would be possible to elect deacons if there are those who are qualified to fill these posts.

It is important to hold as closely as possible to the standards for deacons as outlined in the Scriptures. Acts 6:1-6 and 1 Timothy 3:7-13 will serve as a guide.

It should be understood that the deacons are chosen primarily to relieve the pastor of certain material responsibilities related to the congregation. The New Testament church had elders who served in the spiritual area of church government and ministry. In modern practice, the pastor is usually the only one who is recognized as an elder, unless he has an assistant. In view of this, deacons are often pressed into spiritual responsibilities and must serve as a board of administration in spiritual as well as material things. The matter of church discipline, for example, is usually handled by the pastor and the board of deacons.

The new church should probably hold a business meeting once a year to confirm the pastor, or call a new one, and to elect the official board. As the church becomes more established and the deacons have more experience, they may be elected for three-year terms. Some churches have found it helpful to terminate the positions on different years. For example, a three-deacon board the first time would be elected in this way: One deacon for a three-year term, another deacon for a two-year term, and a third deacon for a one-year term. After that, they are all elected for three-year terms so that there is never a complete turnover in the membership of the official board in one year. Also, many churches have adopted a policy that permits a deacon to serve for two consecutive three-year terms, after which he must remain inactive for at least one year in order to give other qualified men an opportunity to share in the administration of the church.

The deacon board should meet at least once a month. The pastor is the chairman of the board and may call special meetings when the occasion requires.

In the annual business meeting of the church, a financial report should be given to the congregation of all the financial activity of the church. Major decisions such as acquiring church property should have the approval of the entire congregation in a business meeting, even though it may be necessary to call a special meeting for the purpose.

In business meetings of the church, and in the monthly board meetings, the general procedures of parliamentary law should be followed.

9

The Church in Action

IN THE FIRST CHAPTER, it was pointed out that the church has a three-fold reason for being: to minister to God; to minister to the believers; and to minister to the world in evangelism.

THE CHURCH'S MINISTRY TO GOD

Acts 13 presents a functioning church in Antioch which became a missionary base for the spreading of the gospel to the Gentiles. As they ministered to the Lord, the Holy Spirit told them to set aside Barnabas and Saul for their missionary ministry (v. 2). What does the term "ministered to the Lord," really mean? The underlying concept is that of worship. Jesus said, "The true worshipers shall worship the Father in spirit and in truth: for the Father seeketh such to worship Him" (Jn 4:23). In Romans 12:1, we are told that our reasonable service (or spiritual worship) consists not of offering sacrifices of animals which have been slain, but in the presenting of our bodies as a living sacrifice to God. In other words, spiritual worship does not consist simply in the observance of religious rituals, but in the presentation of our life in service to God. Our consecration to God is an acceptable spiritual worship. Worship also includes thanksgiving and praise to God and adoration in which we recognize God's majesty and worth (Heb 13:15-16). We are told that giving our gifts to God constitutes a form of spiritual sacrifice that pleases God (Phil 4:18). Also, doing good and serving humanity is a service or an act of worship to God.

It is necessary for us to realize that the function of the church in worship is carried on not only when the congregation is in the church building, but takes place every day as Christians render service to God in prayer, in their offerings, and in their service to humanity. Servants are exhorted to serve their masters, not as menpleasers, but as servants of God doing the will of God from the heart (Eph 6:6), so that even humble household duties performed with the purpose of pleasing God become an act of worship. There is also worship in a corporate sense when the church is assembled. Evidently the Antioch church was engaged in this type of spiritual service when the Holy Spirit spoke to the congregation (Ac 13:1-2).

It is the function of the church leadership to stimulate an atmosphere of true worship. Worship does not consist of the mechanical singing of hymns or the saying of prayers. These activities may become an expression of worship, but if they are performed mechanically and routinely their performance does not constitute true worship. Jesus said that the worship must be performed in spirit and in truth. The heart must be involved; there must be sincerity and a true desire to draw near to God. Moreover, it takes more than human effort to constitute true worship. The Holy Spirit must inspire and guide us in our worship. Paul tells us that through Christ we have access in one Spirit unto the Father (Eph 2:18). Again, we are told that we cannot pray as we ought "but the Spirit itself maketh intercession for us . . . according to the will of God" (Ro 8:26-27). To attain true spiritual worship is the highest function of the church.

THE CHURCH'S MINISTRY TO BELIEVERS

This ministry is both quantitative and qualitative. That is, the ministry of the church builds itself up in numbers and also in spiritual strength by maturing the spiritual life of the individual members. Several different passages give emphasis to this ministry. Ephesians 4:15-16 points out that Christ is the Head of the body, and its members help each other mutually by the operation of each member so that the individual and the entire church are built up in love. The entire chapter of 1 Corinthians 12 is devoted to the concept of the individual Christian as a member of the body of Christ, and the contribution that each member can make to the whole.

The church is built up by love (1 Co 13) and by the exercise of spiritual gifts (1 Co 12:4-7). There follows then a list of spiritual gifts by which the church is built up and strengthened (1 Co 12:8-31; cf. Ro 12:4-10). Some edify the church by prophecy, exhortation, service, and teaching. The principal ministries to the church (apostles, prophets, evangelists, pastors and teachers) are for the purpose of preparing or "perfecting of the saints for the work of the ministry, for the edifying of the body of Christ" (Eph 4:11-13).

Prayer and intercession for the needs of our fellow believers contribute to the strength of the different members of the church, and consequently the edification of the church itself (Eph 6:18-20; Ro 8:26-27).

The service to the fellow members of the body of Christ is enjoined as a way of edifying the body of Christ. "Do good to all men, especially those of the household of faith" (Gal 6:10).

THE CHURCH'S MINISTRY TO THE UNCONVERTED WORLD

Evangelism has always been, and continues to be the supreme mission of the church. It is commanded by Christ to preach the gospel to every creature and to all nations (Lk 24:47; Mt 28:16-20; Mk 16:15).

The coming of the Holy Spirit was to grant power to believers to become witnesses to all nations (Ac 1:8).

A valid example and pattern is given by the early Christians who "went everywhere preaching the Word" (Ac 8:4). The testimony of the apostle Paul was that he "taught publicly, and from house to house, testifying both to the Jews and also to the Greeks, repentance toward God, and faith toward our Lord Jesus Christ (Ac 20:20-21).

As the closing days of this age approach God has commanded the church to finish the task of total world evangelism. With the immense increase of population throughout the world, it is required that we use every legitimate means for spreading the gospel.

The first and foremost means of spreading the gospel has always been, and will always be, the personal witness of Christians in their contacts with the unconverted. This effort can be backed up by the distribution of gospel literature, evangelism by radio, campaigns for mass evangelism, open-air evangelism in the streets and parks, and evangelistic centers in ghettos and suburbs of the cities.

Each congregation should consider that the unevangelized people in the area are its particular responsibility. Each congregation is responsible to take the gospel message to the territory contingent to its base, at least halfway to the next congregation.

One of the first steps should be a survey of the area in order to find the open doors for witness. These may be simply the opportunity to preach in a home of a believer, or to hold a gospel service in the open air in a nearby village. The church leaders then assign faithful lay workers to witness weekly in each place. A branch Sunday school should be established, with teachers from the mother church helping in this important outreach of their local church. Evening services should be initiated. As converts are won, the process of teaching must be commenced to prepare the new group for baptism. Eventually the outstation can be organized as a church, so that again the process of outreach and church planting is repeated. This system of church extension is effective in cities as well as in rural area. Like a strawberry plant sends out its runners and produces new plants until the area is filled, so the establishing of new churches by means of lay preachers and outstations is a nonspectacular, but effective way to plant churches at the grass roots level.

We have seen this method used in a city with such success that a city with a beginning of 12 new churches, within 10 years had multiplied until there were 40. This same method in a rural area, coupled with a training program for workers, has produced 100 churches within a radius of 30 miles of the central city.

Emphasis must be continually placed on the participation of the total body of believers in evangelism. Great spiritual awakenings are always characterized by the zealous witnessing and fervent prayer participation by the body of Christian believers. As a revival loses its original impetus, the tendency is to place more responsibility in the hands of a few leaders. The activities tend to move out of the homes, the streets, and the open air, and into the church building. The pastor assumes more and more the responsibility for evangelism until the congregation's activity is mostly that of spectators. Thus the evangelistic activity of the church tends to stagnate.

In order to keep the church growing and expanding, every effort must be made to keep the congregation involved at the very center of evangelistic outreach. This means that constant emphasis must be placed on the day by day participation of witnessing laymen. The leaders must see to it that the local church program provides opportunities for such involvement. A good motto: Every church a growing church with every member a witness.

Methods and equipment will not take the place of the Holy Spirit. In order for evangelism to be effective it must be carried on with divine enablement. Nevertheless, the church has before it today open doors of which past generations did not even dream. We have modern transportation that enables us to reach the remotest parts of the world. The printing press, radio, television, and public address systems can all be used to speed the eternal gospel of Jesus Christ. Coupled with this, God has sent His Spirit to give spiritual enablement to His church. The church must take seriously its commission to fulfill its God-given task in today's world.

10

Self-Continuity Functions

WE HAVE SEEN that the reason-for-being functions of the church are to worship and glorify God, to build up the church, and to evangelize the world. These functions must be kept primary. There are also self-continuity functions in which a church must engage in order to carry out the reason-for-being functions. These have to do with the administration of the church, including assignments, finances, buildings, equipment, and discipline. Then, in addition to the reason-for-being and self-continuity functions, there may be auxiliary functions. For example, a program to provide social life for the young people of the church is neither a reason-for-being, nor a self-continuity function, but rather an auxiliary function. This is not to say that such a function is not helpful.

A problem arises when self-continuity functions or auxiliary functions substitute the reason-for-being function. For example, the church must support its pastor in order to carry on its work. This is a self-continuity function. However, should the pastor begin to consider that the main function of the church is to provide his support, then, in his mind at least, the self-continuity function has become a reason-for-being and is substituting the true function of the church. Self-continuity functions are necessary, but must be kept in their proper place.

Administration is one of the necessary self-continuity functions of the church. The church requires the oversight of a pastor and official board, with heads for the Sunday school, youth work, and other ministries, in order that the main objectives of the church may be achieved. To carry out these administrative functions, procedures should be established to coordinate the different areas of responsibility. The pastor should meet with the official board at regular intervals to discuss current problems and opportunities. Assignments may be required for special tasks, problems of personal conflict among workers must be solved, decisions must be reached about the property, and there may be matters of finance or discipline of members to be considered.

The pastor should meet with the official board at least once a month. A regular agenda (list of matters to be considered) should be drawn up, and each member of the committee should have the opportunity of placing any item on the agenda that he wishes to bring up for discussion. The discussion should be carried on in a businesslike manner, with attention given to parliamentary procedures; and each person should be urged to express his opinion. A vote should be taken on each matter, and the results recorded in the minutes.

The pastor should seek a unanimous opinion on every important matter before the board. Care should be taken that no one person dominates the conversation or makes the decision for the rest. A business meeting of the official board is in reality a spiritual function. The meeting should be conducted in the spirit of Christ, and those participating should seek the guidance of the Holy Spirit in the decisions which must be made.

The finances of the church come within the area of administration. The raising of finances is a self-continuity function. The church must develop financial resources in order to carry on its work. The pastor should be supported, church buildings paid for, evangelistic efforts maintained, and missionary projects financed.

The financial help of the church depends largely on the instruction given to the church members at the time that they are brought into membership. There is no better system for the financing of the work of God than the biblical method of individuals tithing their income to the church treasury. Many churches are hindered by lack of an adequate income, and this is often due to the lack of proper teaching of new converts.

Also, it is the responsibility of the church leadership to determine how the finances are to be used. In this area, the support of the pastor normally takes priority. However, a pastor should not maintain that all of the income of the church belongs to him, or even that all of the tithes are his for his own personal support. It may be necessary to employ all of the tithes for the support of the pastor in a small struggling church, but as the congregation increases in size, the tithes should far exceed the personal needs of the pastor. Therefore, it should be understood from the beginning that the tithes of the church come under the supervision of the church board and are not the exclusive personal domain of the pastor.

There should be a system of financial reports to the congregation. A clear understanding of how church finances are handled produces confidence in the membership. When the members know that the finances are being taken care of, they are likely to cooperate with the church more faithfully with their tithes. However, it must follow that the church has a vision for all of the aspects of needs where finances are involved. Otherwise, certain avenues of Christian service are likely to be overlooked with the result that some of the members may feel that they should hold back their offerings and tithes in order to help personally those neglected areas of Christian service. Therefore, the church's financial plan must include not only the self-continuity functions, such as the support of the pastor and the needs of the building, but also the evangelistic outreach and the missionary responsibility of the church. Besides this, the Scriptures teach us that the church has responsibilities for the needs of those who are unable to finance their own living, such as elderly widows. Paul specifically states that those who have relatives should not become chargeable to the church, but the Christian community does have a responsibility to aid those of their number who are no longer able to take care of themselves (1 Ti 5:16). A financial report should be given at least once a year to the church. Some churches also make a quarterly or monthly financial report.

Administrative responsibilities include the care and supervision of buildings. The church leadership should plan ahead for the needs of the congregation so that adequate Sunday school rooms are provided and there is an adequate auditorium for the congregation.

Another area of administration is in the matter of discipline of church membership, but this will be dealt with in a later chapter.

11

A Praying Church

THE IMPORTANCE OF PRAYER in establishing a church and maintaining its spiritual life can scarcely be overestimated. Prayer links pastor and people with the living Head of the church. We are colaborers together with God. Prayer makes this partnership a reality and releases the resources of God to enable the church to carry out its ministry.

Prayer has been called the spiritual thermometer of the church. Some have said that the spiritual strength of the church can be gauged by the number of people who attend the weekly prayer meeting. Numbers, of course, are important, but this by itself is not enough. We must also take into account the fervency and the spiritual power of the prayers. There is a remarkable church in existence in Seoul, Korea. This has come into existence largely through the ministry of Pastor Cho Yonggi. This church has a membership of 8,000 people and its evangelistic outreach is extensive throughout the whole city and the surrounding areas. Pastor Cho has followed the custom established at the time of the Korean revival at the beginning of this century. Every morning before daybreak some 200 to 450 people meet together for an hour of prayer before going to their daily work. Is it any wonder that the church maintains a constant atmosphere of revival with a strong evangelistic outreach?

To pray is to talk with God. Praise and thanksgiving form an important part of prayer. The Psalms provide inspiration and guidance for our prayers. Intermingled with petition are outbursts of praise to God.

Petition is an important element in prayer. Many needs related to our material life often press in upon us, and we can find relief only in presenting our request to our heavenly Father who "knoweth that ye have need of all these things" (Mt 6:32). But prayer is more than petition. The basic aspect of prayer should be communion. This means that it is two-way communication. We talk to God, but we also listen for God to talk to us. Prayer should be accompanied by meditation on the Scriptures, for the Bible is God's voice to us. While the Spirit may speak to us directly, most often He will do it through the Word, and *always* in harmony with the Word. Prayer also includes intercession for the needs of others. In this way we minister to the body of Christ.

What should the church pray for? The Lord's prayer serves as a model. There is more benefit to be derived from the Lord's prayer than simply repeating it from memory. Rather, we should realize the different forms of petitions that are presented and include them in our own prayers.

First there is praise and glory attributed to the name of God: "Hallowed be thy name" (Mt 6:9). Then there is prayer that God's kingdom will come to earth. This is the prayer that God's righteousness will be manifested now through Christian people and that finally the Lord Jesus Himself shall return and establish the kingdom of God upon the earth. There is an acknowledgment of the will of God as being the highest good: "Thy will be done" (Mt 6:10). God's will is accomplished through faith and surrender to His highest purposes. Physical needs are not forgotten: "Give us this day our daily bread" (Mt 6:11). This petition opens the door to present to God our material needs. Then follow the presentation of spiritual needs: "Forgive us our debts, . . . lead us not into temptation, . . . and deliver us from evil" (Mt 6:12-13).

Jesus Himself told us that we should pray for workers in the great harvest field of the earth and indicates that, in answer to prayer, workers will be thrust forth into the field (Mt 9:37-38).

We are instructed to pray for whatever we need to know so as to do the will of God (Jn 15:7-8; 1 Jn 5:14-15). We have the direct statement of Jesus that God will grant whatever will glorify Him (Jn 14:13). Through Christ we can come boldly to God with such requests (Heb 4:14-16). Paul the apostle time and again asked for the prayers of God's people for his ministry (Eph 6:19) and that he be delivered from his adversaries (2 Th 3:1-2).

The needs of others should be a motive for prayer (Eph 6:18). Paul repeatedly tells of his prayers for the churches that he had raised up, that his converts might be strong in the faith. And prayer is to be made for all men, as well, that they might come to know the truth (1 Ti 2:1-4).

Finally, prayer is a mighty factor in reviving the people of God and in extending His kingdom. Turning to the Old Testament prophecy of Joel 2 where an outpouring of the Spirit is promised for the last days, we see also that instruction is given as to the steps that God's people should take in preparing for the outpouring of the Spirit. In Joel 2:12 God calls upon His people to turn to Him with all of their hearts. This means the putting away of every evil thing from the lives of the Christians. There is to be deep humility, with weeping and fasting and a rending of the heart. This means that as the children of God turn from their evil ways and turn to God, a deep sense of their unworthiness comes upon them and self-complacency is banished. Then in verses 15 and 16 the call is made to bring the people together for a united prayer meeting to seek God.

Corporate prayer depends on praying individuals. We cannot be a praying church without having praying people! Even so, the united prayer of God's people adds a new dimension to individual prayer. Something is accomplished by people coming together in prayer that is not always obtainable when individuals pray alone. United prayer seems to compound the power and benefit of individual praying. It is not by accident that all of the disciples were "with one accord in one place" on the day of Pentecost when the Spirit descended upon them (Ac 2:1).

Finally there is an exhortation that the ministers of the Lord should weep between the porch and the altar and call upon God to spare and pardon His people. This is intercession. The priests were to minister between the place where the people stood and the altar of sacrifice. This means that Christians, as a kingdom of priests, stand between a needy people and the sacrifice of Christ on Calvary, asking that pardon and grace may be extended. Every church has a group of friends and relatives who are away from God. What a challenge to pray!

Jonathan Goforth, at a conference at Princeton in 1917, told how a great revival came to Korea. This revival continued unabated for many years, sweeping thousands into the kingdom of God and producing strong spiritual churches.

For months the Presbyterian and Methodist missionaries at Ping Yang had met in daily prayer for revival. This culminated with a special week of prayer in the mother church. It was hoped that God would begin to manifest Himself during

this special week of prayer, but seemingly their prayers went
unanswered.

On the last evening, the 1,500 persons present were startled
when the leading man of the church, Elder Keel, stood up
and said that God could not bless them because of his sin. At
the request of a dying friend, he had agreed to administer his
estate. But in doing so he had kept back a large sum of
money for himself. After confessing his sin, he said that he
was going to give the money back to that widow the next day.

> Instantly it was realized that the barriers had fallen and
> that God the Holy One had come. Conviction of sin swept
> the audience. The service commenced at seven o'clock Sun-
> day evening, and did not end until two o'clock Monday
> morning, yet during all that time dozens were standing
> weeping, awaiting their turn to confess.[1]

Mr. Swallen, one of the missionaries at Ping Yang, com-
mented on the results of the revival:

> "It paid well to have spent several months in prayer, for
> when God the Holy Spirit came He accomplished more in
> half a day then all of us missionaries could have accom-
> plished in half a year. In less than two months more than
> two thousand heathen were converted."[2]

The revival continued to sweep over the church in Korea
during the following years:

> The revival began in 1903. . . . By the middle of 1907,
> there were 30,000 converts connected with the Ping Yang
> center.
>
> It was clear that the revival had not died down by 1910,
> for in October of that year 4,000 were baptized in one week.[3]

1. Jonathan Goforth, "The Spirit's Fire in Korea," in *The Victorious Life*
(Philadelphia: Brd. of Mgrs. of Victorious Life Conf., 1918), p. 185.
2. Ibid., p. 187.
3. Ibid., pp. 187, 188.

What happened at Ping Yang has happened time and again all around the world in many different churches during the twentieth century. As Christians let the Holy Spirit search their souls He reveals the hindrances to revival. When Christians confess their sins and make things right with God and man, God can use them for His glory. Revival comes, prayers are answered, souls are saved, and the church is built up.

12

A Disciplined Church

GOD IS A GOD OF ORDER. He established order in the universe, in the family, in the nation of Israel, and in the church. As a heavenly Father, He disciplines His children (Heb 12:5-11). Jesus gave instructions as to how to deal with erring brethren (Mt 18:15-18). In the midst of the abundant blessings bestowed upon the early church, it was necessary for discipline to be exercised in the problem of Ananias and Sapphira. In this case, God meted out the discipline through Peter (Ac 5:1-11). Paul found it necessary to deal with immorality in the Corinthian church (1 Co 5; see also 2 Th 3:6, 11, 15; Ro 16:17, 18).

THE PURPOSE OF DISCIPLINE

Discipline should not be considered as a punishment on the part of a church. The purpose of discipline is positive and has for its objective the manifestation of the grace of God and the restoration of the person that has committed a fault. The purposes of discipline may be listed as follows:
1. To correct a wrong situation (2 Co 7:8-9)
2. To restore the fallen one (Gal 6:1; Mt 6:14-15)
3. To maintain the good testimony of the church (1 Ti 3:7)

71

4. To warn other members so that they do not become careless (1 Co 5:6-7)

OCCASIONS THAT REQUIRE DISCIPLINE

Discipline should be applied when members are guilty of disorderly conduct. This refers to offenses such as laziness and gossiping (2 Th 3:11-15). Then Paul deals in particular with an instance of flagrant immorality in the Corinthian church (1 Co 5). A contentious and divisive spirit is also given as grounds for discipline (Ro 16:17-18). The teaching of false doctrine must also be dealt with (1 Ti 6:3-5; Titus 3:10-11).

THE METHOD OF DISCIPLINE

Jesus gave guidelines as to how a believer who has committed a fault should be dealt with. When it is possible, the difficulty should be taken care of between the persons who are involved. If this personal encounter does not solve the difficulty, two or three others should be called in to help get to the root of the matter. If the person that has committed the fault still refuses to humble himself, the matter should be brought to the attention of the church, and if he still does not hear, he should be removed from the fellowship. The purpose is to appeal to the conscience of the offender and, by the action taken, make him ashamed of his conduct so that he will repent (Mt 18:15-18). The church is expressly commanded not to treat such as enemies (2 Th 3:15). Jesus said that he should be treated as a Gentile or a publican, which suggested to Jewish believers that he should be excluded from fellowship. Rather than treating such a one as an enemy, we should try to win him back to God (Ja 5:19-20).

We are told in Galatians 6:1 that the task of restoring an offender should be the responsibility of "those who are spiritual." These would correspond to the two or three witnesses mentioned in Matthew 18:15-18. In today's practice, this would be done by the official board of the church or by a special committee for discipline chosen for a special case.

It is important to note that unfounded rumors are not to be used as evidence and that the accusation must be proved by witnesses (2 Co 13:1; 1 Ti 5:19-20).

Should he persist in wrongdoing, he is to be excluded from the fellowship (Mt 18:18; 2 Th 3:14; 1 Co 5:11).

If the guilty party humbles himself and repents, he should be pardoned (Gal 6:1-2; 2 Co 2:7).

If the offender's sin has been of such a nature as to bring reproach upon the testimony of the church, it may be necessary to limit his privileges as a member in order to give time for the public and the church brethren to reestablish their confidence in him. For example, if previously he had led the singing or taken a prominent part in the services, his restoration to fellowship would not mean that he would immediately reassume the same privileges that he had before. To do so would be interpreted by outsiders and by church members that it is a light thing to sin and bring disgrace to the church of God. In some churches, a member is considered on trial for a time and during this time is not permitted to partake of the Lord's supper. The reason is not that he is not worthy before God, but rather because in some areas, especially where the Roman Catholic church is predominant, the partaking of the Lord's supper signifies complete restoration to church fellowship. Therefore they feel that the person who has fallen into sin, such as drunkenness or immorality, must not be permitted to share in the symbolic Christian fellowship of the Lord's supper until the sincerity of his repentance has been proved.

It is important that discipline be not applied secretly but

that the church know what has happened. Otherwise the effect on the guilty person of having to endure the disapproval of his fellow believers for his unChristian acts is lost.

THE SPIRIT OF DISCIPLINE

Discipline should not be considered a punishment, but must be administered in the spirit of meekness and love (Gal 6:1). We must remember that the purpose of discipline is to redeem and to restore. Anything that savors of retaliation is a carnal spirit and disqualifies the person from participating in disciplinary action. The good Shepherd gives His life for His sheep. He is anxious to bring back the wandering one.

Discipline must also be done without partiality. There must be the same severity with the most influential members of the congregation as with the most insignificant.

Discipline should never become a tool in the hand of a pastor or leader to secure his own will. To threaten members with expulsion from the church in order to whip them into line is most reprehensible. Pastors are not to be dictators but guides and examples of the flock (1 Pe 5:1-3).

13

Developing Leadership

IT IS SELF-EVIDENT that a church must produce its own leaders. This is necessary both for natural and spiritual reasons. The natural reasons are that differences in climate, customs, and language may make it difficult for a worker from the outside to fit in. The more primitive the culture, the greater the barrier will be to introduce a pastor from another section of the country. Even in the tiny Central American republics, we have found that workers from one area of the country often find it difficult to adapt themselves to the climate and customs of another section.

Spiritually, it is unthinkable that the church in one area should find it necessary to depend on imported workers. This does not mean that the workers developed in one local church must always stay within that church and become the leaders there, but rather, that one of the important ministries of a church is to produce leaders.

Too often we have limited our concept of the pastor's task in ministry to the church. Some have felt that the pastor has fulfilled his ministry when he evangelizes and wins souls for Christ. Other pastors have seen that it is necessary not only to evangelize but to establish the new converts and mature them in Christian character so that they become useful to

the kingdom of God. Only a comparatively few pastors seem
to realize that an important part of the ministry is to prepare
future ministers for the work of God.

Paul emphasized this ministry when he said to Timothy,
"The things that thou hast heard of me among many witnesses, the same commit thou to faithful men, who shall be
able to teach others also" (2 Ti 2:2).

Jesus chose His disciples, not only to have those to whom
he could entrust His teaching, but to prepare them to become
apostles and transmit it to others. Paul trained Timothy and
Titus among others. The very nature of the church as the
body of Christ indicates that it would produce the leadership
that it needs in any given area.

Every local church should be considered a seedbed that
produces Christian workers. In order to attain this, it is necessary that the pastor have a deep desire to develop leadership
in his church. This whole matter is deeply affected by the
attitude, spiritual maturity, and vision of the pastor. Some
pastors appear reluctant to develop leadership for fear that
a rival to their own authority may result. Others are selfish
in their outlook and want to keep their own church strong to
the extent that they are unwilling for their young men to
leave the local church to train for the ministry. Their vision
is for a strong local church under their own leadership, rather
than that of a church that is witnessing to its community and
producing leaders. There are a few pastors who have a special gift for developing leadership. They know how to inspire
the men with whom they work and to delegate responsibility
to them. This is one of the greatest abilities that a pastor can
develop. A pastor who knows how to put men to work will
usually have a happy, **growing, united** church. A pastor who
tries to suppress **leadership and insists** on doing everything

himself may find that he must struggle constantly to keep down opposition.

Pastors should be encouraged to think of their church as a training center. We learn by doing. The Sunday school, the young people's group, the men's fellowship, outstations, street meetings, and visitation programs all provide opportunities for on-the-job training which can be used to develop spiritual dynamic leadership.

It is a mistake to think that ministerial training begins in a Bible school. The normal and logical place to begin to train workers is in the local church. In fact, there are groups where the total concept of church leadership is limited to what can be produced in the local church. The Assemblies of God of Brazil have worked brilliantly along this line. The elders of the local church are put in charge of outstations, called congregations. These congregations often develop to several hundred in attendance. They acquire their own buildings and carry on evangelistic and teaching ministries. This method develops a strong evangelistic outreach and produces an army of workers. Regretfully, it is weak in the area of formal Bible training, for opportunities for in-depth, systematic Bible studies are very limited. In recent years, Bible institutes have been established to help correct this weakness.

The ideal workers' training program includes a strong activity program in the local church, coupled with specialized training in systematic Bible teaching such as is available in a Bible institute. The church in each country should develop a broad-based training program. It is not enough to choose a few men and give them highly specialized training to become pastors. It is essential that training be given on every level, and this should include the training of local workers as well as specialized training for those who aspire to full-time ministry.

Above all, our training in Bible institutes should be kept practical. The intellectual and theological preparation must be coupled with a practical evangelistic outreach. Here is where many theological institutions have failed. They have taught their students courses such as theology, church history, and public speaking, in an atmosphere almost entirely divorced from the day-by-day living of the people to whom they are to minister. The recent emphasis on theological training by extension is at least a partial answer to this need. Theological training by extension aims at giving at least a portion of the necessary studies to the students in their own area rather than limiting such training to what can be obtained in a regular seminary program. The theological school should have a vigorous evangelistic outreach, and the students should be given the opportunity to engage in practical aspects of ministry in outstation, and on the streets, as well as in the pulpits of the churches.

The future of every national church depends on the quality of the workers that the churches produce. There is no more important aspect in the life of the church than that of the preparation of its future leadership.

14

The Local Church and the Church Universal

A LOCAL CHURCH represents only one small part of the universal church.

The organization of the local church is set forth in the Scriptures by inspiration of the Holy Spirit. It exists as the agency of God in the community, the local unit of the body of Christ. Even so, it is not an entirely divine institution, for it is made up of fallible men and women.

Local churches do not stand alone, either in relationship to the invisible universal church or in relationship to sister churches established around the world. Particularly those churches which belong to the same tribal or linguistic group, or are established as a result of the effort of a particular group in the same nation, must of necessity have a relationship to one another. This is entirely scriptural for both Luke and Paul spoke of the churches of Asia and the churches of Judea, as though they were a unit (Ac 9:31; 1 Co 16:19).

In our day we do have an obstacle which the early church did not face. Today the Christian church is divided into denominations. The original church lost its purity and power and drifted into the Dark Ages. As there was a recovery of spiritual truth, the evangelicals broke away from the Roman Catholic church. Then, among the Protestants, as different Biblical truths were rediscovered, not all enjoyed the same degree of understanding, so that those receiving this light often found it necessary to separate from the parent body. Often this action was forced upon them. It should be realized that many of the divisions that exist in the Protestant world today represent a struggle for truth. While divisions in Protestantism are regrettable, yet, even this is to be preferred to the union in ignorance and error of the Middle Ages. Beyond the divisions of doctrine and organization, the great majority of true Christians recognize their spiritual union with other people who have been born of the Spirit of God, quite apart from their denominational affiliation.

In the same way that an individual Christian should not remain isolated, but find fellowship, edification, and protection as a member of a local church, so a local church should not remain completely isolated from sister churches for its own edification. Also, a greater degree of stability is usually experienced when a church is not left entirely to its own devices but has the support and fellowship of other groups of like precious faith. Another benefit is the protection that such affiliation affords. When a church is entirely isolated, it can more easily fall victim to false teachers and wolves that come to prey upon the flock for their own ends.

Finally, one of the greatest benefits in an affiliation of association of churches with one another is the fact that together they can carry out projects of evangelism, educational projects, benevolent enterprises, and the training of national workers. One church alone could never accomplish many of these objectives; by joining with other local churches in a common purpose, these goals can be achieved.

Such an association of churches must have a common basis

of fellowship. The basis of scriptural doctrine is of supreme importance here. We cannot walk together unless we be agreed. We would beg for tolerance in nonessentials. Some things are too insignificant to merit a rupture of fellowship. Other doctrines may be divisive and harmful. The apostles said, "Avoid them" (Ro 16:17). In order for true unity to exist and for the fellowship of the churches to be meaningful, there must be an accepted standard of doctrine and practice. This will cover the basic doctrines of the churches and become the basis for recognizing new groups as well as for approving workers.[1]

Usually when there are three or four churches formed in a country or tribe it is time to draw these churches together in an association or conference for their mutual edification and protection. It is to be remembered that any kind of national or sectional organization that exists grows out of the churches for the purpose of helping the churches and of extending their work rather than to bind them with restrictions. In other words, the national organization serves the constituency. Supervising committees formed are responsible to the churches and should exercise care that they do not invade the churches' scriptural prerogatives. The usual way to form the association is by delegates chosen from each of the local groups together with their pastors who together form a representative group for the churches to guide the development of the work.

There are two extremes to be avoided in this matter of the association of churches. First, any extreme attitude of independence which would fail to recognize the spiritual union that exists between the members of the body of Christ. We are free in Christ, but we are not independent! The other extreme to be avoided is that of developing a strong central-

1. See fn. 2, p. 46.

ized hierarchy which will arbitrarily assume authority in matters that pertain to local churches. This is an abuse of the scriptural pattern.

An organization or association of churches and ministers is needed particularly for the purpose of approving ministers who may be given the right hand of fellowship among the churches. There is a great need for objective scrutiny of those who desire to enter the ministry. Standards of conduct and doctrine must be established, and there must be a meaningful way to show disapproval toward someone who fails to maintain the high standard of the church.

The local church should be made aware of the doctrines and practices of the association. The churches should loyally support the fellowship for the benefit of all and not selfishly retain an isolationist position. The local church should assume its proper financial share in maintaining the organization and contributing to its approved projects.

A word here is in order concerning our relationship to evangelical churches and Christians of other denominations. Of course, denominational churches were unknown to the New Testament period. Today they represent a fact of church life. While denominationalism is to be regretted inasmuch as it often affects adversely the unity of the Body of Christ, yet it is not entirely without advantages. For one thing, there is less danger of the church becoming a monolithic structure, such as occurred in the centuries that followed the apostolic area and resulted in one central universal authority. Perhaps denominationalism, even with all its evils, is to be preferred to a repetition of that experience.

Also, it could be that God is using the multiplicity of denominations and mission structures to hasten the task of world evangelism. Thereby neglected regions are entered and thousands reached, many of which probably would not hear the gospel without these different bases for evangelistic thrusts. The danger comes when the Christian assumes that his group is the only true group and that the body of Christ is limited to the people of his own denomination.

We must recognize the universal aspect of the church of Jesus Christ. God sees the true church as one, belonging to the one Head and given life by one Spirit (Eph 4:4-6). We should be more than ready to reach across denominational lines and extend the hand of Christian fellowship to every true child of God whose life is in harmony with the gospel witness. Since the church is all one body, we should cooperate with other Christian groups in reaching the lost for Christ. This does not mean that we have to compromise our own doctrinal positions or give up those methods that the Holy Spirit has guided us to use. Nor does it mean that we are forced to acknowledge as a brother professing Christians who are not living in accordance with the precepts of the gospel, or to open our doors to false workers and provide them an opportunity to scatter our flocks. It does mean that we must try to see things from God's viewpoint, open our hearts to His children regardless of denomination, and endeavor to rise above parochial outlook which would shut out from our Christian fellowship those who are truly children of God but wear other denominational labels.

15

Social Responsibility of the Church

THE CHURCH is primarily a spiritual entity, a union of men and women who have been born anew by the Spirit of God, and thus become the body of Christ in the earth, representatives of the kingdom of God. The church's objectives and ministries are primarily spiritual. However, the local church is made up of individuals and families who are bound together in a common faith and purpose. Thus, the church is also a social entity. Individuals and families relate to each other within the church, which becomes a Christian society. These relationships bring with them responsibilities.

The church's social responsibility begins with its own members. This came to light early in the history of the primitive church when the apostles were faced with the responsibility of caring for the widows among their number (Ac 6:1-3). Paul charges that the church should take care of widows who have no other means of support (1 Ti 5:3, 5). At the same time, he insisted that when believing widows had children or nephews who were able to take care of them, that the church should not be made chargeable (1 Ti 5:4, 16). The same ruling would naturally be applied to orphans.

Also, there are instructions to Christians concerning those who find themselves destitute (Ja 2:15-16). The appeal, in this case is made primarily to Christians as individuals to share their goods with the needy.

The church should do what it can to relieve the suffering of its own members. Some churches have a commissary to provide food and clothing for those who for some reason are left destitute. Other churches maintain a benevolence fund to which all the members contribute to help those in special need. All local churches should study their problems and take steps to set up funds and administration to care for those in need.

At the same time, strong injunctions are given to individuals that they should not look to the church to supply their material needs, but rather that each one should work to provide for himself and perhaps share with others (Eph 4:28).

It will be recalled that the Gentile churches took up special offerings to help the Christians in Judea when famine struck that area (Ac 11:27-30; 2 Co 8:1-6; 9:6; 1 Co 16:1-2).

Some churches find it possible and necessary to provide schooling for their children, and some have visiting nurses that care for the sick.

This generosity of the church extends also toward the unconverted. "As we have therefore opportunity, let us do good unto all men, especially unto them who are of the household of faith" (Gal 6:10). Jesus told his disciples to "Let your light so shine before men, that they may see your good works, and glorify your father which is in heaven" (Mt 5:16). The true Christian with the love of God in his heart will do all that he can to help those in need. Jesus gave practical teaching of this in the parable of the good Samaritan (Lk 10:30-37). The law of love, "Thou shalt love . . . thy neighbor as thyself" (Lk 10:27), inspires the Christian to relieve suffering and to help those in need.

THE CHURCH AND POLITICAL STRUCTURES

What is the relationship of a church to the political structures in the country where the church is located? Some insist
that in view of the fact that the political systems are corrupt,
oppressing the people instead of serving them, the church is
obligated to join in political revolution. These people base
their argument on the fact that the prophets in the Old Testament spoke out against wicked rulers and condemned their
practices. They also appeal to the fact that the Christian
must stand for social justice, and the only way to do that ef-
fectively is to stand with those who are attempting to over-
throw the present order. This is becoming a divisive issue in
many Protestant circles. What should our stand be?

It should be a Christian stand. What was Christ's attitude
in this matter? What did the early Christians do about it?

We should call attention to the fact that neither on the
local nor on a national level was the church intended to be a
political entity. Although as a spiritual body it has social
responsibilities, the church was never instructed to accomplish its goals through politics or through violent revolution.
Jesus told Pilate simply, "My kingdom is not of this world"
(Jn 18:36). Jesus, in His intercessory prayer, said, "They
[the disciples] are not of the world, even as I am not of the
world" (Jn 17:16). When, in one instance, He was appealed
to for social justice in the matter of the division of property,
He refused to take the place of a judge. "Man, who made me
a judge or a divider over you?" (Lk 12:14). When He was
asked to take a stand against paying taxes to the Roman government, which was considered unjust and unpatriotic by the
Jews, He answered "Render therefore unto Caesar the things
which be Caesar's, and unto God the things which be God's"
(Lk 20:25).

Certainly, the Roman Empire with the dictatorship of the Caesars presented a sad picture of political and social oppression. Slavery was everywhere. Yet both Paul and Peter urged obedience to the governmental powers (Ro 13:1-7; 1 Pe 2:13-15). Slaves were told to render service to their masters as servants of Christ (Eph 6:5). The Christians were considered to be a spiritual force—the salt of the earth. The objective of Christianity is not primarily to change social structures, but to change men. At best, the most equitable form of government in the world is corrupted and becomes oppressive when those people who are in charge are selfish and non-Christian. The poorest form of political government can be beneficial to the people if the men are the right kind of men. It is a utopian dream to believe that revolutions can produce social justice in the earth without change in the hearts of men. True Christians long for social justice and peace on the earth. However, this is not to be brought about by the revolutionary activity of the church in politics, but by the coming of Christ to reign on the earth. In the meantime, the task of the church is to form that nucleus of born-again men who belong to the kingdom of God.

The influence of Christian men does change communities and nations. We have been eyewitnesses of this change. People are changed by the gospel and no longer live in drunkenness—robbing and killing—since Christ has come into their hearts. A little of this kind of salt seasons the whole community and changes the social climate. The Christian conscience at work has brought about great changes in society. These are by-products of the gospel. In Chile, a great number of the common people have been reached by the gospel of Christ. Their services are sought by employers because they are known to be honest, and they come to work on Monday morning instead of staying home to sleep off a hangover! By the same token, as the gospel comes into the lives of people, they want their children to become educated and to have a better life. There is no greater contribution that the church can make to the social structure than to preach the gospel of redemption from sin and to see lives transformed.

All this does not mean that a Christian can be oblivious and indifferent to oppression that may exist around him. The Christian will let his voice be heard on the side of justice and use his vote to the best of his ability to bring about change. The Christian may acept an office in government when he feels that such a position can help him serve his community. However, he will refrain from joining subversive groups. There are two reasons for this. One is that it has been shown by experience that men who join in subversive groups, even with the objective of obtaining good for their country, invariably lose out spiritually. The atmosphere of conspiracy and rebellion is a death warrant to true spirituality.

Second, the church is not a political entity, and Christians are ill-prepared to know whether the subversive group that they are asked to join will really produce benefit for the country. Many evangelicals felt that Castro was a real deliverer for the Cuban nation, and they joined enthusiastically in the movement. Pastors took their places on the platform with Castro's men and publicly espoused the revolution. What happened? It divided the churches. In the pastors' congregations were people who had relatives killed in the Castro movement. In such circumstances the unity of the church suffers, for it is not likely that all Christians will have the same political opinions. Later the pastors woke up to the realization that they had made a terrible mistake. Instead of liberty, greater oppression came. Evangelical churches and schools were closed, and the task of carrying on the gospel was made infinitely more difficult.

We must remember that we are now in the final stages of God's program upon the earth. God is seeking out people for His name who will be true followers of Jesus Christ (Ac 15:14). There is coming a time when Christ shall reign. Peter said that "we . . . look for new heavens and a new earth, wherein dwelleth righteousness" (2 Pe 3:13). In the meantime we must preach Christ and His gospel. We must show love to all men and work for the coming of that kingdom which is the answer to the earth's ills.

16

The Church in Mission

"Go ye therefore and teach all nations" (Mt 28:19). A true Christian is a member of the universal church. Every local church is a unit of the body of Christ, and a representative of the universal church. The accident of geography does not change this vital truth. It is equally true in South America as in Europe, in Africa as in North America. As Christians who have received the knowledge of the gospel, we are debtors to those who have not had this opportunity. We are in their debt whether they live next door to us or on the other side of the globe! (Ro 1:14).

As a new local church is established, the privileges and responsibilities of this worldwide fellowship should be held before the new group. Every church should have the satisfaction of being a participant in world evangelism. Every Christian should become aware that he is a debtor and learn how to discharge his debt.

There was a time when young churches in the newly evangelized lands were content to receive missionaries. To them the idea of a missionary was a person who came from Europe or North America. This is no longer so. Chilean churches are sending missionaries to Argentina, and those in Brazil are sending missionaries to Bolivia and Paraguay. Korea is sending missionaries to Indo-China, and African tribes are being evangelized by Christians from other tribes. The task of world evangelism is too great to be limited to any one mission, or to any group of select people who carry the name of missionaries. If the harvest is to be reached throughout the world in our time, it must be done through the cooperative vision and effort of all the small local churches everywhere with the participation of every Christian in the challenging task of world evangelism.

When a church is founded, it should begin as a missionary church. Every church must realize that it does not exist simply to enjoy the graces and blessing of God for itself, but to share. Every pastor should seek to instill a missionary vision in the congregation. A missionary vision can be imparted by encouraging the Christians to pray for the harvest fields of the earth. The words of Jesus command us to do this. "The harvest truly is plenteous, but the laborers are few; pray ye therefore the Lord of the harvest, that He will send forth laborers into His harvest" (Mt 9:37-38). We cannot earnestly pray for a need without becoming personally involved.

Then, we must encourage a missionary vision in the church by giving them information about the mission fields of the earth. When Jesus was facing the missionary opportunities of the Samaritan village, He said to His disciples, "Look on the fields; for they are white already to harvest" (Jn 4:35). Pastors cannot, of course, stand at the edge of a village in a far-off land and look literally on the fields, but they can give their people a vision of the missionary needs in various ways. They can gather reports of God's working in other areas of the earth, and share them with the congregation. Letters from workers in far-off areas will serve to stimulate missionary interest. The headquarters offices can furnish reports of missionary work being done in new areas of the country. An informed people will be a concerned people.

In every church there should be an established custom of receiving a missionary offering at regular intervals. A congregation may follow any plan it desires in carrying this out. However, it should be a consistent and unselfish effort. Probably once a month is ideal for most churches. Every Christian and every church needs to feel that it is making a contribution to the work of God beyond its own local area. In this way we share the universal fellowship of the mission of the church.

Another great contribution that a church can make is to encourage the young people to open their hearts to the call of God for His work in carrying the gospel to the ends of the earth. If the church has its own young people engaged in pioneer evangelism or church planting they indeed feel more of a part of this universal mission.

The missionary program of the national organization should begin at home and reach out to the ends of the earth. We have Acts 1:8 to guide us here: "Ye shall be witnesses unto me both in Jerusalem, and in all Judea, and in Samaria, and unto the uttermost part of the earth." We begin at our Jerusalem with the founding of the local church. We should not be unconcerned about the neighboring villages and cities in our Judea (province). Missions is not only for the ends of the earth, but it is for the next province also.

Finally, countries in no way related to our own land should be included in the program. In some countries missionary funds, which are made up from the contributions of all the churches, are divided between efforts within the country and foreign projects, with seventy-five percent of the money being used within the country itself, and the other twenty-five percent designated for missionary projects in other lands outside of its own borders. Missionary projects could include helping a worker to go into a new field and start a church. There should be some help for travel and setting up housekeeping. Probably some support will be allocated for a limited time until the work can become established.

Some churches make the expenses of training workers in their Bible school a part of their missionary program. They realize that they cannot carry the gospel to new areas of the country without prepared workers. This is good, but it should not be the total missionary program of the church.

The churches in some countries are sending missionaries to other countries on a permanent basis. It is understood that they are not going abroad to take pastorates, but to evangelize and establish churches. Therefore, they must have continual support. Once again, the national organization must assume the responsibility of endorsing the workers and of deciding what help can be given.

With the demographic explosion around the world, the harvest is greater today than ever before. The doors are open. We have the promise that when the gospel is preached as a witness to all the nations, the end shall come. A glorious opportunity with weighty responsibility challenges the church of our day. Let's go forward into all the earth until Christ returns.

17

Summary

HERE THEN are the principal emphases in church planting. God's program for today is a church planting program. He has indicated that He will accomplish His purposes for the world in this present epoch through the church.

Evangelism is a primary and indispensable mission of the church. This requires that wholehearted continuous effort be made to win men to Christ. God carries out His purposes through individuals who have been personally transformed by His redemptive power.

A principal channel for this evangelism is the local churches, properly instructed in the Scriptures, and guided by leaders of vision in their outreach to an unconverted world.

Coupled with the place of the local churches in evangelism is the importance of lay participation in the evangelistic thrust. Every member should be a witness and a worker.

The message preached must be biblically based, and Christ-centered with emphasis on the reality of divine intervention in human affairs.

Human instrumentality is important, but it must be remembered that it is no more than that—an instrument. God Himself is the author of church planting. The presence and power of the Holy Spirit are as indispensable today as in the first

94

century of the history of the church. "Be filled with the Spirit" (Eph 5:18).

Finally, the challenge to the church in today's world is to be in reality *the church*, fulfilling its commission to carry this witness to every creature in the nation and to every nation under heaven.

DATE DUE

DEC 1978			
DEC 14 '81			
1-5-82			